# This is Me!

Written by Charlotte Guillain
Illustrated by Katriona Chapman

## Collins

11

# Making a picture

# Ideas for reading

Written by Clare Dowdall, PhD
*Lecturer and Primary Literacy Consultant*

**Learning objectives:** show an understanding of how information can be found in non-fiction texts to answer questions about where, who, why and how; use talk to organise, sequence and clarify thinking, ideas, feelings and events; extend their vocabulary, exploring the meaning and sounds of new words; hear and say sounds in the order in which they occur

**Curriculum links:** Creative Development: Exploring media and materials

**High frequency words:** this, is, me

**Interest words:** picture

**Resources:** whiteboard, mirrors, pencils and sketch paper, collage materials to make self portrait

## Getting started

- Give children some mirrors and ask them to describe themselves to a partner. Support children's vocabulary, e.g. *I have short, curly hair.*

- Look at the front cover and read the title, pointing to each word. Ask children what the girl has done, e.g. made a picture of herself.

- Read the blurb together, pointing to each word. Encourage children to join in with familiar words.

- Ask children to suggest how the girl has made the picture, and what materials she needed.

## Reading and responding

- Ask children if this will be a story book or an information book. Explain that the book will tell them how to do something and give them information.

- Look at pp2-3 together. Ask children to describe what the girl is doing. Give children time to look at themselves in their mirrors again. Introduce the word *features.*